WATER
IN THE
GARDEN

F

FRANCES LINCOLN LIMITED
PUBLISHERS

WATER
IN THE
GARDEN

ANDI CLEVELY

PHOTOGRAPHY BY
STEVEN WOOSTER

Water in the Garden
Copyright © Frances Lincoln 2006
Text copyright © Andi Clevely 2006
Photographs copyright
© Steven Wooster 2006

First Frances Lincoln edition: 2007

Andi Clevely has asserted his right to
be identified as the author of this
work in accordance with the
Copyright, Designs and Patents Act
1988 (UK).

A catalogue record for this book is
available from the British Library.

ISBN 10: 0-7112-2641-5
ISBN 13: 978-0-7112-2641-8

Printed and bound in Singapore

9 8 7 6 5 4 3 2 1

Water is a fertile resource for
gardeners, whether it provides a home
for distinctive aquatic plants like these
water lilies (page 1), drips lazily from a
sparkling curtain of weighted chains
(page 2), or gushes in a lively torrent
over a broad stone ledge (this page).

CONTENTS

INTRODUCTION

Water and life

Life began in water. It often appears to be everywhere: it covers about seven-tenths of the world's surface, although only 1 per cent of this is fresh water. Most plants are two-thirds water, which is essential to keep them upright and in active, healthy growth. And gardeners are often heard to complain that it never seems to stop raining.

Inexhaustible, even adequate supplies of water are not universal, however, and never have been. Over time many plants have learned to survive in places where periods of drought are endemic by developing strategies such as succulent stems, hairy or waxy leaves, or an annual retreat into hiding as dormant bulbs.

Because natural cycles and life processes throughout the natural world depend so much on water, prolonged shortage can cause serious disruption and injury. In our

Just one of water's many diverse moods and qualities, as a calm reflective pool that is instantly inviting to sit beside for a quiet interlude in the day.

The earliest gardens

Some of the first gardens were made in the Middle East, where heat and drought are routine. Throughout the Islamic Empire water was a precious commodity, to be used sparingly and efficiently. It was often ducted into shaded patios and courtyards, where it was stored in pools or driven through fountains to cool the air. A source of water was in fact a guarantee of a comfortable existence, even a status symbol, and paradise was thought to be a calm refreshing water garden.

Like a window on another world, the surface of still water can mirror ornaments (above) or marginal foliage (right) and magnify their impact.

gardens, for example, plants become lacklustre, limp or leafless, vital soil chemistry slows down and ceases as the moisture content below ground declines, dead material stops decaying and vital systems go into hibernation.

As well as being the original crucible of life – itself an enormous claim to respect – water is essential for sustaining the health and wellbeing of all forms of life on this planet. It makes good sense, then, to use it sensitively and appreciate its qualities, both globally and in the local context of our gardens.

Water's dual character

To gardeners water is both a practical necessity for healthy, vigorous plants and an important design ingredient that can add music and movement to static surroundings in a variety of imaginative ways.

The simplest water feature will supply vitality and enchantment as it moves in ever-changing patterns and rhythms or lies in calm limpid pools, reflecting the sky like a mirror. More complex arrangements are possible, created around a basic closed circuit of moving water that is driven through a sequence of pools and falls by an inexpensive electric pump, with levels kept topped up automatically from a cistern linked to the water mains or from ducted rainwater.

The sides and surroundings of any water feature can be planted up with a host of moisture-loving species,

Relieved of any need to struggle for survival, water plants such as irises are able to concentrate energy into producing gorgeous, sometimes extravagant flowers.

which are often some of the easiest plants to look after: most keep their good health and active growth simply by being near water. More aquatic species live contentedly in or on the water itself, where they need little attention apart from control of their natural tendency to expand. Ponds are usually rich in nutrients because water bearing dissolved plant foods from elsewhere in the garden is liable to run into them, sometimes making a pond too fertile and resulting in temporary problems with algal blooms or 'green water' (see page 106).

The value of water features

For various reasons such as over-cultivation, pollution or retreating water tables many natural ponds and watercourses have disappeared in recent decades – a loss that threatens the survival of a range of pond creatures and wild plants. On the other hand, studies have shown that back gardens are often overlooked as sanctuaries for wildlife, and that garden ponds are an important component of this vast network of habitats.

Soon after a new pond or watercourse is filled, you are likely to have visits from birds, water beetles and even dragonflies; later it will probably host water boatmen, caddis fly larvae, tadpoles and even pond plants that have been transported as seeds or live fragments on birds' feet. Accept these as recognition of the value of your creation and appreciation of your providing a congenial site for them.

Safety matters

Treat water with respect, especially where small children are concerned. They must always be supervised near water. Larger ponds should be enclosed to a height of 90cm (3ft) with a childproof fence, or covered at or just below the surface with a grille of 8mm ($\frac{3}{8}$in) welded mesh. Alternatively limit your plans for a few years to a simple bubble fountain or small waterfall that is switched on only while the children are supervised. Teach older children a basic code of good conduct when near a pond, both for their own safety and to prevent them from disturbing its inhabitants.

This immediate acceptance by wildlife alone would be sufficient justification for introducing a water feature into your garden. But children and adults alike are also irresistibly drawn to water (see box) and enjoy watching or touching it, or simply being near this amiable and benevolent element that can provide rare opportunities for play, rejuvenation, reflection and relaxation.

THE NATURE of WATER

Water is easily undervalued, especially wherever an apparently inexhaustible clean, fresh supply is available on tap, and it has often been squandered, taken for granted or polluted. Gardeners probably appreciate more than most people that it is in fact a precious resource, one to be managed efficiently to avoid waste but also capable of being used creatively in features that can calm or beguile with their beauty and playfulness.

Extremes of scale: a generous and well-stocked pond (previous pages) for water lilies, which demand plenty of space, compared with beauty in a basin (left), where an intimate feature has been created from a combination of subtle lighting, simple pondweed and running water circulating through an old brass tap.

HOW WATER BEHAVES

Although at first sight just a simple and unexciting liquid, water has extraordinary, almost magical properties that make it unique in the natural world.

Water shapes our world. Over long periods it can wear away the hardest rock, sculpt the landscape and eventually produce the soil in our gardens.

Water can dissolve a great variety of substances: it supplies all the food materials for plants in a liquid form that the roots can absorb. It can also carry waste materials and surplus chemicals like fertilizers into ponds and streams. It can store huge amounts of heat without changing its temperature, so water bodies like ponds can moderate extreme heat and cold, stabilizing the temperature and making the surroundings feel more comfortable. Most liquids shrink when they freeze, but water expands as it becomes ice, so ice floats and ponds freeze from the top downwards. In the coldest weather the bottom of a deep pond is about 4°C (40°F), allowing fish and dormant plants to survive under the ice.

The water cycle

Clouds deliver water to the ground as rain, which collects and flows downhill in streams and rivers until it meets the sea; there it is evaporated by wind and sunshine to become the water vapour of clouds once more. Even in countries with a reliable piped water supply to homes, this simple water cycle decides where and when rain will fall and whether there will be enough for our needs. With the increasingly unpredictable influence of climate change, gardeners need to collect and conserve water (pages 16–17) against times of shortage: installing a water feature is one particularly valuable and ornamental method.

USING WATER IN THE GARDEN

Successful gardening depends on the wise and frugal use of water. Beds, borders and containers are huge reservoirs of water, which fills most of the spaces between the particles of soil and compost. This soil water is absorbed by plant roots and steadily passed into the atmosphere through plants' foliage, which can lose as much as 25 litres per sq.m (5½ gallons per sq.yd) every week. Wind and sunshine can evaporate much more from the soil itself.

Whether deliberately pumped round a circuit or arriving intermittently as ducted rainfall, water can be collected for storage in drums that double as reservoirs and whimsical sculpture.

This rapid depletion of soil moisture in the growing season is the reason active plants require regular and sometimes frequent watering. However, you can reduce the need for this by conserving water in a variety of ways:

Add organic matter Materials such as compost and manure worked into the soil annually will rot to form humus, a spongy material that absorbs and stores huge amounts of water. Spreading more on the surface as a mulch reduces the evaporation of soil moisture.

Collect rainfall Water butts linked to downpipes from gutters can hold large amounts: connect several, each receiving the overflow from its neighbour, with the last overflow directing surplus water into a pond.

Store water underground When building a moving water feature that uses a pump to circulate water from a buried reservoir, consider excavating enough space for a larger water tank that can be kept topped up with rainwater.

Waste household water

Clean waste water – from rinsing or 'running the tap', say – can be collected in a bowl for adding to a pond or water butt. The contents of a bath and other forms of 'grey' water should never be added to a pond, where soap and detergent residues cause problems, but they may be used to water plants in an emergency (soil bacteria can neutralize small amounts of waste matter quickly). A more efficient and decorative method is to pass grey water through a series of two or three linked settlement ponds planted up with reeds (*Typha* and *Phragmites* species): these filter out impurities and then discharge cleaned water into the final pond.

Water wisely Soaking the soil around individual thirsty plants with a can is the most precise way to water; irrigate larger areas with seep hoses (perforated irrigation pipes) laid between plants. Do not use sprinklers, which are indiscriminate and waste water as spray drift.

Match plants to sites Different plants have evolved to cope with specific conditions and grow best where conditions resemble those they have adapted to. Moisture-loving plants thrive in wet soils and bog gardens, for example, while desert and Mediterranean species survive on hot dry sites without regular watering.

Stone and water are perfect partners, in formal combination as a terrace swimming pool (left) or in a more naturalistic setting, with relatively small amounts of water gently descending a flight of stone steps (right).

THE PLEASURES OF WATER

As well as contributing to the efficient use of water in the garden, features like ponds and streams provide unlimited delight, entertainment and even comfort. On a hot day, for example, the atmosphere is cooler and more refreshing near any water feature, especially where water splashes or bubbles, filling the air with invigorating negative ions. Depending on the available space you can create a tiny feature such as a bubble fountain for intimate, safe enjoyment or major installations such as a reed-bed filtration system to recycle domestic grey water, a pond for growing edible plants (page 21) or even a natural swimming pond (see box).

Water has personality and moods that can be used to transform the feel and appearance of your garden. Try to define early on exactly what appeals to you about water and what qualities you expect it to contribute. Since installing any water work involves a lot of time and careful effort, and the result will be a permanent – possibly prominent – feature, plan now to avoid disappointment.

A pond to swim in

A swimming pond looks like a large natural garden pond but consists of two distinct zones: a central part, about half the total area and deep enough for swimming, and a shallower surrounding margin where aquatic plants purify and regenerate the water without the use of chemicals such as chlorine. The result is a beautiful and low-maintenance pond that is attractive to wildlife and swimmers alike, does not compromise the environment like a conventional swimming pool, and can even be heated with solar panels.

The existing layout and atmosphere can help you choose the best way to incorporate water into your garden. For example, a lush wildlife pool would look incongruous beside immaculate annual bedding but would nestle comfortably into a wildflower corner, while a cool angular cistern with tiled surround might complement a contemporary courtyard but seem out of character in a cottage garden.

Decide if you want the lively sound and movement of a cascade or waterfall, or just still water to reflect the sky and add cool tranquillity on a summer's day; somewhere for a few fish and specimen aquatic plants or a semi-wild pool teeming with underwater creatures and dragonflies overhead.

As stone landscapes reveal after rain, any depression can become a water world, whether temporarily in a superficial stone hollow or more lavishly in a spacious garden rock pool.

Natural models

As you contemplate the various kinds of water feature and start to assess which is likely to suit your plans and the nature of the site, consider some of the natural examples around you and the lessons that can be learned from them.

Water is always on the move in the natural world, working its way downhill in search of the lowest point. In steeper country a stream bubbles up as a spring or gathers rainfall draining from surrounding land, and flows fast over a stony bed, tumbling over rock ledges as waterfalls. Its turbulent passage keeps the water clean and sweet: algae has no chance of developing because dissolved nutrients are few, plants are discouraged from rooting and constant motion helps the water absorb purifying oxygen. The key characteristics of a young natural stream are rock and stone, lively movement and noise, clarity and freshness.

Garden counterparts are waterfalls, cascades, spouts and fountains.

In middle and old age streams flow over much gentler lowland gradients. Their speed slackens, so they do not scour the bedrock clean. Soil deposits accumulate and plants can establish themselves – both streamside species along the banks and aquatic plants out in the deeper water. Many of these are oxygenating plants, which help maintain water quality. In built-up areas a stream is often forced to flow in a culvert, its naturally wayward course confined in a symmetrical and disciplined channel where little grows.

In the garden these stages are represented by plant-rich water gardens and formal canals and channels.

When flowing water meets a barrier it gathers in a static pool wherever there is a hollow with an impervious bed; this fills until the stream overflows and resumes its downward course. This feature may be nothing more than a temporary puddle, a free-standing pond fed by a stream or drainage water running off the surrounding ground, or a deeper part of the stream bed where the water pauses before flowing over the edge as a waterfall. In these calm conditions plants and algae establish easily in varying ratios that decide whether the pond is airless and stagnant or a healthy balanced home for wildlife creatures like diving beetles, tadpoles and fish. Other water-loving plants colonize the damp banks and soggy surroundings.

Garden examples are bowls, basins, bog gardens and all the different kinds of pond.

A pond for food plants

In various cultures growing edible crops in ponds is an established practice, and even the smallest pond can be productive, making it an ideal feature for allotments and kitchen gardens; as a favourite habitat for toads, it can also help in the control of slugs and other plant pests. Many water lilies have edible roots and leaf stalks, while almost all parts of the lotus (*Nelumbo* spp.) can be eaten. Marginal plants such as watercress, arrowhead (*Sagittaria*), common reeds (*Phragmites communis*), reed mace (*Typha*), water mint and sweet flag (*Acorus calamus*) all have edible leaves, stems, flowers or rhizomes.

MAKING YOUR CHOICE

The range of water features is enormous, and you will need to balance aspirations, feasibility and the character of the site to help you select the best kind. Moving water features are more costly and complex to install than a simple pond, but you can always add one later as an extension to an established pond. Or it may be more practical to construct several complementary water features at the same time to create a varied and satisfying wetland scene. Whatever you choose you are unlikely to regret inviting water into your garden.

BUILDING a POND

The key component of most water gardens is a pond, the simplest kind of wetland site and probably the most adaptable. Occurring naturally wherever water collects and is prevented from draining away, it is the most straightforward to build and requires no knowledge of hydrology. All you need to do is find or dig a hollow, make it waterproof and then fill it with water. The rest is detail and decoration.

INSPIRATIONS

There are many reasons why you might want to build a pond in your garden. Perhaps you want somewhere to keep a collection of fish or need to cool a hot patio or courtyard in summer. You may already have a damp, low-lying part of the garden where nothing but sedges and rushes seem to grow; or you could be lucky enough to have a stream running through your land. If you want to encourage wildlife where you can watch it unobtrusively, a pond is a guaranteed attraction for a range of creatures. Whatever your reasons, you need to keep them clearly in mind, because they can help you decide the pond's position and style.

Sources of ideas are equally varied. A visit to a garden centre or established garden can spur you into dreaming, or you might have been inspired by natural water and wetland features to recreate something similar closer to home. Like many others you might simply be entranced by the many moods and qualities of water, and want to include these in the garden's repertoire because of their soothing or uplifting effect on your own senses and wellbeing.

Possibly the most versatile element in garden design, water is equally fitting as a soft ingredient in a sophisticated built landscape (previous pages) and when used to supply a specialized habitat in lushly planted surroundings (left).

STYLES

Whatever its purpose, a pond will be either formal or informal in appearance.

The classic role of water as the cool centrepiece of a courtyard, collected in a cruciform raised pool animated by gentle bubble fountains and flanked by slim sentinels of Italian cypress (*Cupressus sempervirens*).

Formal ponds

These are quite self-consciously man-made and rarely pretend to imitate any kind of natural feature. They tend to be geometrical in shape and centrally or prominently placed as key features, perhaps enhanced with formal accessories like a classic fountain. Planting is restrained or minimal, but ornamental fish are entirely appropriate.

Ponds may be sunk at soil or deck level or raised above ground; an indoor pond in a conservatory or greenhouse is usually a formal raised structure. Although Oriental ponds (see page 34) commonly include landscape elements, they are designed according to strict guidelines and are generally regarded as formal.

Left Stony inlets, broad-leaved marginals like hostas and gently sloping turf banks are informal ingredients which help create an ideal wildlife habitat.

Right Mellow recycled brick edging and a 'found' log feature relieve the angularity of this otherwise formal lily pond.

Informal ponds

These are intended to be more naturalistic and are very appealing when well made, but they need skill if they are to look totally plausible. The most relaxed kind is often designed to attract and sustain wildlife (page 37). Many informal designs are a successful compromise, setting an irregular, boldly planted pond in deliberate contrast to formal hard-landscaped surroundings. Natural ponds need more space than formal designs, however, as well as more care to help them blend convincingly into their garden setting. They are often combined with a waterfall or similar active feature; any planting areas can be extended or developed into a bog garden or rock garden.

PLANNING

Choosing a site

Garden features such as a patio or lawn can be conceived indoors on paper, but when planning a pond you often need to start with the site and develop the scheme from there. This is less critical for a formal

A cleverly contrived garden wetland that blends authentic elements such as reed bed, natural pond and bog garden into an informal landscape where marginal and moisture-loving plants can flourish unchecked.

Waterlogged ground

This may be a boon if it means you can simply dig out a hollow that fills naturally and remains full all year, especially as doing this might also improve the drainage of the rest of the garden. On very heavy clay soil you may able to 'puddle' the pond bottom (page 44). If you plan to use a flexible liner or pre-formed unit, however, the site will need draining because an existing high water table can exert pressure from below, distorting or dislodging the structure.

pond, which may be intended to embellish an existing area, but natural ponds need siting in likely places where they look uncontrived.

The lowest part of the garden where you would expect water to drain naturally according to the terrain is a potential site – the contours of your garden might even suggest a possible watercourse to run into or from the pond. Any area that regularly lies wet, perhaps where sedges or rushes grow lushly in the grass, is a suitable candidate, although it might be easier to turn it into a bog garden (page 102) because building a pond on waterlogged land can sometimes lead to problems (see box).

Where no obvious site suggests itself choose the most appropriate place with the following criteria in mind.

Sunlight is essential for good water quality and plant health – most aquatic plants need at least six hours' sunshine daily in summer. Make sure that buildings do not cast heavy shade for long periods during the day; and avoid overhanging trees, however charming they might look – as well as shading the pond, their fallen

foliage can sink and foul the water.

Avoid extreme sites. Although a pool will pleasantly cool and relieve hot airless areas, the water can evaporate quickly, you will need to oxygenate fish to avoid stress and the temperature of shallow water can fluctuate wildly. Exposure to wind lowers temperatures and increases evaporation; cold air trapped in a frost hollow can cause a pond to freeze for long periods.

Assess any proposed site from all angles, not just outdoors but as a view from the house: any kind of water feature has an almost mesmeric quality and will inevitably draw attention to itself wherever it can be glimpsed. Positioning a wildlife site where it is easily and quietly watched from indoors can help to avoid alarming pond visitors.

A perfect example of the way in which lush groupings of bold marginal and bog garden plants can balance the otherwise assertive geometry of a formal pool, timber-decked platforms and connecting bridge.

Check the surroundings for potential problems or danger. Tree roots impede excavation and can grow through pond liners, and tree species such as horse chestnut, laburnum and conifers will contaminate the water and possibly kill fish. Make sure you know the whereabouts of drains and buried water pipes and electricity cables; proximity to an accessible electricity supply may be an advantage, however, if your plans include a pump or lighting installation.

Access can be important for various reasons and you may need to make a path to the site, possibly running around the perimeter. Convenient access will be essential during construction, especially if you are using a contractor with machinery. All but the most natural ponds may need topping up in summer, so accessibility to a tap or hosepipe is important, and routine maintenance is easier where there is room to manoeuvre – when dividing marginal plants or tackling problems with algae, for example.

DESIGNING THE POND

Balance is paramount, both within and around the pond, and timidity and over-ambition are dangers equally to be avoided. Planning the largest pond the site can accommodate might give its ecosystem greater stability but costs can become excessive and the result could easily dominate the rest of the garden. On the other hand a tiny shallow pool can dry out quickly and may look inadequate unless you feel a simple formal scheme suits the garden as a whole.

Stand in the proposed site and try to visualize the pond's appearance from all sides, in winter when planted surroundings might be bare and in summer when the area is full of growth. Consider the volume of soil that might need removal: will you excavate this yourself or employ a contractor, and where will the spoil go? Decide whether you are likely to extend the pond in the future to include other water features, planted areas or decking for relaxing at the waterside.

Then mark out a tentative shape on the ground, using rope or hosepipe for irregular shapes, pegs and string for formal straight-sided designs. Measure the area so that you can estimate quantities of materials and costs, and try modifying the outline while you are still at the early planning stage to see if you can improve on the original scheme or perhaps make economies.

Calculating size

- The size of a proposed pond will be affected by its purpose as well as its location.
- Goldfish need 0.09 sq.m (1 sq.ft) of surface area for every 5cm (2in) of body length.
- Koi carp prefer a minimum depth of 1.2m (4ft).
- Many water lilies require about 2 sq.m (22 sq.ft) of surface for good growth.
- A minimum depth of 45cm (18in) in part of the pond is essential for a healthy ecosystem and freedom from freezing.

Practical factors for formal ponds

Simple symmetrical shapes have the most impact and can either echo those near by or make a stylish contrast with them – an oval in a square deck, for example.

Straight sides running parallel to strong features like house and garden walls look classical, but you could align them at an angle for a challenging disparity.

Consider interlocking shapes for variety or extreme shapes to create illusions: a long narrow pool can alter the apparent dimensions of a garden, for example.

Plan to use materials that imitate or complement their surroundings. Formal ponds extend the built landscape, so their visual correspondence is often an important part of their appeal.

Designed to complement a courtyard setting for dining and entertaining, this formal water feature supplies sound and movement with concealed lighting for after-dark atmosphere and a broad tiled edge where visitors can sit and trail their fingers in the water.

Practical factors for informal ponds

Avoid sharp angles and straight lines: informal is free form, but not so fussy that the outline looks like an aimless doodle.

Keep variations gentle for an authentic look and remember that the natural action of water tends to soften or obliterate detail.

The pond needs to integrate, either with the lie of the land, like a dewpond, or, if it is to be planted, with nearby beds and borders. Include submerged shelves for baskets of marginal plants.

Simple shapes provide the greatest surface area, increasing the pond's reflective impact and its potential for planting or stocking; complex outlines increase the length of edging that might need finishing and integrating.

Making a final plan

When you feel you have considered all the options and decided on a design, you need to set your ideas down on paper.

First sketch the relevant area of the garden, adding all the main features and boundaries, and measure critical distances so that you can transfer all the information to a plan drawn to scale on squared paper. Make several photocopies if you still need to experiment with alternative ideas.

Add the outline of the pond, at first in pencil to allow you to change or modify the details. Annotate the plan

Water is a key ingredient in many Oriental gardens, as here, where it tumbles and flows across the centre of a rocky composition in classic imitation of a natural landscape.

Oriental ponds

Although formal in concept, the ideal Oriental pond is placed slightly out of the way and surrounded by carefully selected worn rocks and pockets for a few choice specimen plants. Water depth is not as important as a large placid surface area designed to reflect the sky or important nearby features – a tree or pleasing view of the house, for example.

with features like proposed plantings, the position of a pump with the course of its attendant pipework and cables, and perhaps accessories such as seating or lighting features. Add all these to the same scale to make sure that sizes and distances are realistic. When you are satisfied with the result mark up a final copy as a working diagram.

This recycled galvanized steel tank makes a satisfying still water feature but illustrates the need for careful installation to ensure a perfectly level surface.

MARKING OUT

You are now ready to transfer your plan to the chosen site as a full-size layout. This is still provisional and you can make adjustments as you go if space or existing features and contours suggest changes. Remember to mark these revisions on your plan, especially if someone else is to carry out the work.

How you mark out the ground depends on the method of construction you choose. Most designs can be drawn on the ground with dry sand trickled from a plastic bag with one corner removed. If the area is turfed, a hosepipe or rope can be left in place for a week and will tattoo the ground with a yellow outline.

Strictly formal designs can be marked out with lines and pegs for straight lines; scribe circles with a sharp stick on the end of a line attached to a central peg. Set pre-formed units upside down on the ground and draw round the rim for a precise outline.

Live with this rough design for a few days and further refine if necessary.

Establishing levels

Water is self-levelling and will always betray any inconsistencies by overflowing or exposing part of the pond side. To establish levels you will need a number of sharpened pegs, a club hammer, a spirit level and a straight board long enough to straddle the pond.

Drive the first peg into the ground slightly outside the marked outline so that its top is just above ground level, and identify it clearly as the reference or 'datum' level. Insert further pegs at regular intervals all round the outline, checking each against its neighbour with the spirit level. When you have completed the perimeter, confirm your levels by testing a board resting diagonally from corner to corner or side to side across the pond. You will then have a consistent baseline against which to check depths.

Regulating water levels

Although many gardeners top up a pond with a hosepipe, you might prefer to adjust levels automatically, and you should build a means of doing this into plans before starting work. The usual way is to run mains water to a buried cistern, which is fitted with a ballcock valve and an outlet at the surface of the pond. A falling water level will empty the cistern, causing the ballcock float to drop and open the mains inlet valve. You could also install an overflow pipe from the pond, set just above the outlet from the cistern and leading excess water to a drain, soakaway or bog garden. Fit the pipes through holes in the liner and secure them with self-sealing watertight couplings.

EXCAVATION

Decide well in advance whether the scale of the work justifies hiring a mechanical digger, in which case the best time is summer, while the ground is dry and less easily compacted; if you are digging by hand spring and autumn are more comfortable seasons. Avoid winter when the ground can be wet and heavy or even frozen. Plan where the excavated soil is to go and the easiest route to use.

Skim off any turf and stack this out of the way, either to re-lay later or to rot down as a fibrous soil conditioner.

Dig out the top spit (spade's depth) all over the site and stack this on its own on a heavy plastic sheet. This topsoil is usually too fertile and friable to squander and can be reused when planting and landscaping round the pond.

Continue digging down into the subsoil. Keep this separate from the topsoil and use it to build any slopes or gradients for moving water features.

Test for depth against your pegs and stop when you reach the level of the pond floor. If you are including planting shelves (page 101), stop digging at this intermediate level, mark out the remaining central outline and add a new set of levelling pegs, and then continue digging to the bottom.

THE POND LINER

This basic sequence of operations is the same for all sunken ponds (for raised ponds, see page 45). How you continue or modify the work depends on the material you use to line the pond and make it waterproof. Three kinds of liner are commonly used, each with distinct virtues and disadvantages. All three types need an underlay to keep liner and soil apart and to prevent problems from stones and intrusive roots. If you garden on heavy clay you may not need to line the pond (see page 44).

Allowing plants to spread and colonize pond margins and even creep into the water helps to disguise the inevitably raw edges of a pond liner.

Flexible liner This is the easiest material to lay and readily moulds itself to fit irregular shapes, but it is not so successful for sharp angles and corners. Durability and cost vary according to quality, from polythene – the cheapest but with a very limited life span – to butyl rubber, the toughest and most expensive of all. Sheets are made to measure (see box page 40); for very large ponds two or more sheets need welding together, which is best done by the supplier before dispatch.

Pre-formed liner Moulded units in various sizes and shapes are made from flexible or reinforced plastic or stronger fibreglass. Unlike flexible liners these units are rigid, so the excavation must be carefully conformed to fit and support the liner all round to avoid local stresses and possible cracking. Many designs have a natural finish and include marginal shelves for plants, and there is sometimes a choice of colours for more creative schemes.

Concrete This is very strong and permanent, and easily moulded to your specification, but laying concrete is

Calculating dimensions

Unless your supplier requests otherwise, work out the size of flexible liner you need with this simple formula.

- Measure the maximum depth (D) and double it (2D).
- Measure the maximum length (L) and width (W).
- Allow 45cm (18in) extra for edging at each end and side.
- Sheet size equals L + 2D + 90cm (3ft) long, and W + 2D + 90cm (3ft) wide.

strenuous work and requires skill to do well. Depending on the design you might also need to include reinforcement or to erect shuttering for steep sides. The material is better suited to small formal designs than large natural ponds.

INSTALLATION

Installing a flexible liner

If possible choose a warm day for the work , as then the liner will be more pliable. Liners are usually supplied folded for easy manipulation, but assistance may be useful for adjusting the fit and lie of liners for larger ponds.

❶ Excavate the site 5cm (2in) deeper and larger than the finished size to allow for the underlining. Remove all large and sharp stones and sticks from within the hole and along the edges. Line the hole with a 5cm (2in) layer of builder's sand; use thick newspapers, carpet underlay or loft insulation on steep sides.

❷ Unfold and centre the liner loosely over the hole and anchor it all round with bricks or stones. Slowly run water from a hosepipe into the centre of the pond. As the liner stretches, adjust the stones to help it settle comfortably and mould itself to the pond contours. Fold it neatly to fit corners.

❸ When the pond is full, trim the surplus liner to leave a 45cm (18in) border all round to cover with the chosen edging (see page 48).

Installing a pre-formed liner

Accurate digging is important, although adjustments are possible during installation. Complex shapes need particular care to ensure that the cavity offers consistent support all round and that the unit sits perfectly level in the ground.

❶ Use the mould as a template, first upside down to mark the outline and then right way up to locate the position of the bottom, where the cavity will be deepest. Dig out the hole at least 5cm (2in) deeper and larger all round. Check that the base and any shelves are level.

❷ Remove all stones and sticks, and tread the base of the hole firm. Line the excavation with a 5cm (2in) layer

Although an irregular outline is preferable for increasing the variety of habitats offered, even a simple or symmetrical shape can produce a successful wildlife pond.

of builder's sand, centre the liner in place and test for fit and level. Add more sand where needed until you are satisfied with the fit.

❸ Part fill the unit with water and then backfill any gaps round the sides with fine soil. If the unity is thin and pliable, raise the level of the water and backfilled soil at

Here water is used as an important element in a courtyard plan, as a winding canal to echo the sinuous curves of the brick and tile floor. A hidden pump could generate a gentle flow from end to end.

the same rate to avoid distortion. Test for level once more while the unit is still moveable and then fill the pond completely. Water the backfilled soil and tamp firm.

Installing a concrete liner

Make sure you know how to mix and handle concrete, and consider hiring a mechanical mixer for larger quantities.

Estimating quantities

Concrete is calculated by volume in cubic metres or yards.

- Measure the surface area of the floor, sides and shelves in square metres or yards, and add all these figures together.
- Multiply the result by the thickness of the concrete: if 10cm (4in) thick, for example, multiply by 0.1 to give cubic metres or $1/9$ for cubic yards.

❶ Excavate the hole 15cm (6in) deeper and larger all round. Make sure the sides are no steeper than 45 degrees to prevent the wet mortar from slumping. Tamp level surfaces firm and then line the hole with heavy-duty polythene, damp newspapers or carpet underlay. Cover this lining with 5cm- (2in-) mesh wire netting, overlapping any joins by 10–15cm (4–6in), and tread in place.

❷ Mix up concrete, using 4 parts 15mm (³⁄₄in) gravel, 2 parts builder's sand and 1 part cement (all measured dry with a bucket or shovel), plus an optional waterproofing additive. Spread this evenly 10cm (4in) thick over the mesh. Cover with sacking if frost, heavy rain or hot sun (dampen the sacking) are expected, and leave for three weeks.

❸ Mix a finishing coat of 4 parts builder's sand and 1 part cement (and waterproofing compound if used) and spread this 5cm (2in) thick, smoothing the surface with a float for an even finish. Protect from weather and leave for ten to fourteen days.

❹ Paint the surface with concrete sealant to prevent lime from leaching into the water, leave to dry (24–48 hours) and then fill the pond with water

CLAY PONDS

Once the standard way to make a farm pond was to drive cattle through a natural wet hollow to compact or 'puddle' the clay bottom and make it waterproof.

Although simple and effective (many of these ponds have survived for centuries), it is a difficult method for garden ponds except where the soil is naturally heavy. On lighter ground sticky clay can be bought in for spreading and consolidating, while dried granular clay is available in bags for mixing with water to the right consistency for making a lining. Artificial clay ponds are easily damaged by tree roots and hot weather, which can dry and crack exposed areas, but the method is particularly suited to making a bog garden (see page 102).

If your soil is naturally heavy and sticky try digging out a shallow-sided depression. Wait until the exposed clay is saturated with winter rain or soak it yourself for several hours: the clay is ready if a handful can be squeezed and rolled into a ball or sausage shape that does not fall apart. Tread the level surfaces until they are very solid – enlisting the help of friends and children can make this operation entertaining – and pummel the sides firm with the flat of a spade.

You can then fill the pond with water. If this gradually leaks away, wait until the pond is empty and re-tread all the surfaces. Top up the water level whenever necessary to prevent drying and cracking. To avoid puncturing the puddle, grow plants in baskets, especially deep-rooted reeds and sedges like vigorous *Typha* species.

Constructing a raised pond can save the need for extensive excavation and produce an attractive feature that captures attention and varies finished surface levels.

RAISED PONDS

A raised pond is a practical alternative to digging a ground-level site and is the simplest solution for building on a hard surface like patios, courtyards or an indoor area such as a conservatory. Planting and maintenance are less arduous because less bending is involved, the pond contents are easier to appreciate at close hand, especially for less able people, and the water is more easily drained for cleaning or repair.

The main materials used for excavated ponds – flexible and pre-formed liners and concrete – are all suitable, but these need to be enclosed and supported by a strong and rigid framework of walls. These can be built from stout timber, at least 15 x 10cm (6 x 4in) in section with secure joints, or brickwork that is well bonded and preferably 23cm (9in or 2 bricks) thick. Remember water is heavy (a 10 litre/2 gallon bucketful weighs over 9 kg/20lb), and you might need to build a special foundation raft of 15cm (6in) deep concrete if the existing base is not strong enough.

Almost concealed by luxuriant planting, this metal trough (left) betrays its presence by the sound of water dribbling gently from a wall-pipe, whereas the mosaic cube (right) is a striking and conspicuous centrepiece that immediately draws the eye through the bold gateway.

Flexible and rigid liners should be bedded on sand and cushioned at the sides with a thick layer of underfelt, insulating material or old carpet. Trap the top of the liner neatly under the last course of brickwork or a row of coping stones. Concrete tanks are best made from brickwork rendered inside with waterproof mortar and finished with one or two coats of sealant.

A POND IN A CONTAINER

Small ponds made by filling a watertight container are ideal for confined spaces such as balconies, and as special features for more intimate appreciation – an attractive bowl in which to float flower heads or fragrant oils near where you usually sit, for example, or a wooden tub to house a miniature water lily. This may be your only pond, or you could dispose several in favourite places – water features rarely become repetitive or tedious.

Unless it is to be hidden among plants, choose a container that is appealing even when empty. Make sure it is weatherproof as well as watertight. If intended for

Almost as bizarre as the glowing water column, waxy-flowered *Anthurium andreanum* (left) is an exotic moisture-loving plant for humid indoor pools. Calla lilies (*Zantedeschia aethiopica*, right) are handsome marginals, hardy if grown in 15cm (6in) of water, while *Menyanthes trifoliata* or bog bean (far right) spreads steadily in the shallowest water.

Zinc or copper cisterns and hot-water tanks are ideal for a modern setting (but do not keep fish where they can make contact with copper), or can be clad with brickwork like traditional greenhouse irrigation tanks. An old glazed sink makes an excellent miniature lily pond, especially if its domestic appearance is disguised with a coating of hypertufa – a mortar mix of 2 parts peat or peat substitute, 1 part sand and 1 part cement applied over a tacky priming coat of PVA glue.

FURNISHING THE POND

Edgings
Ground-level ponds need some kind of edging to provide a finished frame, hide the rim of the liner and ensure dry-shod access. The materials you choose should match the pond's style and surroundings.

Paving Slabs, tiles and bricks are all suitable for formal ponds. They should be bedded in mortar for safety, with all their joints tightly grouted. Dig out a shallow shelf all

growing water plants it should hold a minimum of about 27 litres (5 gallons), but smaller containers are ideal for bird baths, floating candles or for a green carpet of tiny pond plants like duckweed or fairy fern.

For long life timber containers can be charred with a blowtorch if otherwise watertight or lined with plastic sheeting secured near the rim if not. Used wooden tubs and barrels made to hold liquids will have panels coopered to a tight fit: filling one of these with water should encourage the wood to swell and seal all the joints.

Do not overlook the potential of other discarded containers that can be recycled or adapted to hold water.

Plants for tiny ponds

There are many naturally non-invasive or slow-growing species, among them bog arum (*Calla palustris*), dwarf horsetails (*Equisetum arvense* and *E. variegatum*), corkscrew rush (*Juncus effusus* 'Spiralis'), bog bean (*Menyanthes trifoliata*), dwarf reedmace (*Typha minima*) and the smallest water lilies: *Nymphaea* 'Aurora', *N.* 'Graziella', *N.* 'Odorata Minor', *N.* 'Pygmaea Alba' and *N. tetragona*.

Plants for indoor ponds

Tender aquatics and marginals normally grown outdoors only in summer can be overwintered or kept all year in a water garden indoors. Examples include papyrus (*Cyperus*), lotus (*Nelumbo*), water lettuce (*Pistia stratiotes*) and water hyacinth (*Eichornia crassipes*). Common houseplants such as alocasias, anthuriums, monstera, pilea, strelitzia, zantedeschia and many ferns enjoy waterside conditions and can give the pond a tropical appearance.

49

Given sufficient space and resources, water can be teamed with a host of landscaping accessories, such as a gravel and brick causeway (top right), the stone pavement and outcrops of a lavish rock garden (bottom right), or a timber platform large enough to be a waterside patio (opposite).

round the perimeter while excavating the pond, so that the paving sits flush with the ground level.

Rocks Parts of an informal pond margin can be edged with natural or artificial rocks for atmosphere, to hide pumps and pipes or to make a rock garden or waterfall. Mortar them firmly in natural groupings.

Turf This makes a sympathetic edging for informal ponds. Use a spade to skim and peel back a margin of existing turf when excavating the pond, so that it can be unrolled over the edge of the liner, or lay new turf when you have finished. Try to prevent lawn mowings from falling in the water and causing pollution.

Decking Both formal and informal ponds can be edged with a walkway made of wooden decking if this is securely laid on strong timber piles or bearers, or firmly bedded concrete blocks. Make sure the surface does not become slippery with algae.

Plants As well as those marginal and aquatic species normally grown on the pond shelf (page 101), there is a rich variety of moisture-loving plants to grow along damp edges, where they will hide the liner and stabilize banks with their roots. Where the soil is drier, almost any garden plant will soften the appearance of the pond margin and reflect on the surface.

51

Artificial lighting exploits the reflective qualities of water to magical effect, whether concealed as spotlights permanently focused on particular features (left) or staged for the occasion as outdoor candles and flares (right).

Lighting

Artificial lighting can enhance the impact of water, prolong its appeal long after dark and contribute an air of mystery or festivity to the surroundings depending on the way it is arranged. A choice of fittings is available:

Spotlights can be placed in or around the pond. Some have spikes to plunge into the soil; others can be floated or attached to walls, focused on particular targets or to subtly illuminate the water.

Floodlights are less discriminating and light up larger areas. They are very effective under water, especially if fixed just below the surface. Fountains can be bought with integral flood- or spot-lighting, often multicoloured with a switching unit to automatically change colours.

Water and light mix well; water and electricity do not. The combination can be lethal if safety guidelines are not followed meticulously. If an electricity supply is already fitted outdoors for the water feature, it may be easy to add wiring for lights; otherwise consult an electrician.

Introducing fish

These are fascinating creatures that contribute colour and animation to a pond. They blend well with most styles and are particularly appealing in formal ponds, but they can prey on a range of water creatures in a wildlife pond, where they are best kept in a separate section to give other forms of life a chance.

Common goldfish are often the most successful and least demanding, and will tolerate relatively shallow or cold water; their fancier forms may need to be overwintered indoors. Orfe and koi carp need larger, deeper ponds with plenty of oxygenating plants (page 96). If your pond is primarily intended for keeping fish,

The cool, calming presence and mirror surface of still water, collected in a simple stone cistern with one or two floating plants and a shoal of bright goldfish.

discuss the project at an early stage with an experienced stockist who can help you provide ideal conditions.

Wait at least six weeks (up to a year in unsealed concrete ponds) after filling to let the water stabilize and any green colouring or cloudiness disperse.

Use a simple pH test kit to determine whether the water is excessively acid (from decaying plant matter and run-off from the garden) or alkaline, usually caused by unsealed concrete or limestone rocks. A buffering agent can be added to the water to adjust readings.

Allow new plants several weeks to settle and establish as scavenging fish can disturb or uproot them. Cover baskets with a gravel mulch to protect the compost.

Introduce new fish gradually. First float them in their bag on the surface, and then add a little pond water to the contents two to three times every ten minutes before finally tipping the bag gently on its side to let the fish swim free.

Catering for pond wildlife

Soon after completion you may notice the first wild arrivals, usually one of the various beetles that regularly fly around

looking for new territory. If your pond is intended to attract wildlife there are several ways to make it more inviting.

Supply mud This is important for a range of creatures that forage or pass some stages of their lifecycle under water. Spread a 10cm (4in) layer of soil on the bottom before filling the pond carefully for the first time.

Add wild organisms A small container of water from a natural pond or stream will often contain a range of organisms, especially if you dredge up a little of the bottom debris. Do not move larger creatures like frogspawn from natural sites.

Grow their favourite plants A number of inviting wildflowers, such as water mint, bog bean, water plantain and brooklime, will enhance your pond without creating a wilderness. Add flat-headed garden flowers like sedums, achillea and chrysanthemums.

Provide buffer zones Areas of taller grass and berried shrubs near the water can supply shelter and forage for a range of species as well as helping the pond blend seamlessly into its surroundings.

3

MOVING WATER

Water in motion has a fascination all its own. At the flick of a switch a well-planned feature will spring to life and animate the most barren environment with light and music, and even simply ducting rainwater can add a hint of impromptu charm to a grey day. The principles are simple, the rules few, but the results can bring magic to the garden.

Water brings vitality to the garden on any scale, whether as a modest trickle from a bamboo spout feeding an improvised pool and bog garden (previous pages) or as a realistic placid stream sliding over a rock bed, complete with densely planted banks and wildlife sculpture (left).

A flowing stream or waterfall has an individuality quite distinct from that of still water, and requires a different approach and management. Moving water must have a source and a destination, for example, and to make it flow from one to the other you need to tap an existing watercourse or build a closed circuit driven by a pump.

MANAGING NATURAL SOURCES

Having a stream running through your garden is cause to rejoice, as it saves you the work of constructing an artificial gradient and system of pipework, plus the installation of a pump and its power supply.

You could leave the stream as it is and concentrate your attention on adapting and planting its margins with moisture-loving plants, or modify the course of the water, perhaps by digging out a header pool as a reservoir to feed other features or by constructing a waterfall in its path.

Natural streams fluctuate with the seasons, however, and you should make allowances in your plans for a possibly reduced flow in summer or a sudden surge after rain. You also need to liaise with local authorities if you propose extracting water from the stream or otherwise altering the volume of water normally flowing from your premises.

PUMPING WATER

All artificial moving water installations require a pump and a power supply.

Streams, waterfalls and similar larger features also need a gradient to flow down and a delivery pipe to the highest point.

Pumps

Circulating water is pump driven. Water is drawn by the pump through a filtered input and then expelled under pressure through an adjustable outlet. This outlet can be coupled directly to a fountain or geyser assembly, or to the end of a delivery pipe if the water is to travel any distance. There are two kinds of pump:

Surface models These are powerful and can move large volumes of water, but they tend to be noisy and need to be housed in a special dry, ventilated chamber. This may be constructed below water level, or above; if the latter, the inlet pipe must be fitted with a foot valve to keep the pump primed (full of water).

Pump capacity

A pump is rated by the quantity of water it can move per minute or hour. To calculate the size you need to:

- Measure the approximate length, depth and width of your watercourse or channel.
- Multiply the three figures together to give an estimated water volume.
- Decide whether you want a torrent or a trickle: if the volume is 500 litres, it will be circulated every ten minutes by a 50 litres (11 gallons) per minute pump or take nearly an hour with a 10 litres (2 gallons) per minute model.
- Measure the vertical distance between top and bottom of the watercourse, as pumps are also rated by the height to which they can lift water.
- Velocity is adjusted by the size and configuration of the stream bed (see page 69).

Submersible pumps These are self-priming, silent in use, relatively inexpensive to buy and easy to set up, making them the best choice for most domestic schemes. They sit under water in a collecting pool at the foot of flowing water gradients or underneath fixtures such as fountains.

Flowing water needs a controlled route through the garden in a style that suits its surroundings, perhaps meandering as a subtly contrived natural stream or, as here, firmly ducted in a formal landscape.

Supplying power

Some very large pumps are driven by petrol or diesel generators, but most garden models are electrically powered. Smaller kinds can operate on a low-voltage (usually 12- or 24-volt) current supplied through a transformer, which is connected to the mains either with a suitable extension lead from indoors for occasional use (see Chapter 2), or to a weatherproof outdoor socket fitted with an RCD (circuit breaker).

Most models work directly off the mains, which may mean fitting a new circuit and connection to the mains consumer unit. This is a job for a professional electrician, who will also supply essential components such as armoured cable and trench conduit where necessary. If you do the wiring yourself it must be checked and approved on completion by an electrician.

A few small pumps suitable for bubble and millstone fountains or wall spouts are solar powered, a simple and sustainable option that avoids the necessity of installing wiring and an external mains circuit. The energy of sunlight is collected by a small solar panel set

unobtrusively in a sunny part of the garden, and converted to electricity. Some features are driven direct and only work in sunshine, but others can store the power in battery cells for use later.

GRADIENTS

Water runs down a gradient, and the speed of its flow depends on the steepness of the slope – a young river tumbles and gushes down a precipitous hillside but slows down in maturity when it reaches the lower levels. For practical purposes the overall slope of a stream course should be ten to thirty degrees above the horizontal. Plan the course so that it contains natural variations, with pools, steep cascade sections or abrupt falls separated by nearly level interludes with smooth, gentle meanders.

When planning gradients try to exploit any existing differences in level to avoid unnecessary earthworks, and remember the need for scale: ambitious schemes can dominate the rest of the garden, inflate the budget and demand large water volumes and powerful pumps. A simple gentle flow of water, perhaps arranged to seep through a stretch of rocks or gravel and then drop from a height into a small pool, can still supply plenty of movement and resonance.

An unadorned channel of softly moving water breaks up and animates this paved patio, and may be fed by rainwater conducted from roof guttering.

The water supply

Water is pumped from the main pool or reservoir at the lowest point up to its source by a delivery hosepipe, the length and height of which will affect the choice of pump. Arranging the pipe to run directly from reservoir to source rather than beside a winding stream course can reduce its length and the demands made on the pump.

The route of the pipe is usually hidden from view, tucked behind rocks and plants or buried in the soil. Its outlet may be similarly disguised above ground (an underwater outlet may siphon the contents out of a header pool), or it can be coupled up to feed a more formal source such as an urn or statue.

The reservoir at the bottom, together with any header pool, should be large enough to prevent a noticeable drop in level when the pump starts working, and to avoid frequent topping up in hot weather. For most schemes a simple plastic tank about 38–45cm (16–18in) square and deep is an adequate reservoir.

Using a filter

Most pumps contain a sponge filter, which is adequate for smaller circuits, but where large volumes of water are being moved it is advisable to install an external filter unit to protect the pump from ingesting harmful matter and to keep the water consistently clear, especially if fish are kept. The filter is attached to the pump inlet and may be mechanical, with the water drawn through an inert material such as gravel or charcoal, or biological, containing a resident population of bacteria that break down any trapped debris. Filter units are rated by the amount of water they can handle, and you should aim for a model that can process at least half the water volume of your system per hour.

CHOOSING A STYLE

There are few constraints that affect planning a moving water feature, especially if you make it with a flexible liner or concrete – these allow more freedom and an appearance of spontaneity than the limited range of pre-formed units (see page 67). The available space and to a certain extent the contours of the land will need to be taken into account, and you should also distinguish between formal and natural styles.

Formal streams

Like pond designs (see page 32) these tend to be geometrical in shape and layout, and often look better if they harmonize with the style and materials of their surroundings. Examples of formal watercourses include rills, which are slender channels that are usually straight or elegantly shaped and laid almost at ground level so that a film of shallow water (no more than about 2.5–4cm/1–1½in deep) moves slowly and peacefully, and canals, which are deeper channels (up to 30cm/12in deep but still narrow enough to step over) set at ground level or on top of a low wall and, again, with the gentlest of falls.

Natural streams

These are harder to design successfully so that they look uncontrived. The course of a natural stream is neither straight and symmetrical (unless culverted), nor

Simple yet effective, this slender canal cutting its unerring way through a lush carpet of ground cover is filled with water that may be static or gently propelled by a small submerged pump.

excessively winding or elaborate. Flowing water erodes the sides of its channel, softening fussy angles and regular outlines, and your design needs to reproduce this look and pretend that the water found its own way through the garden. Remember the affinity between water, stone and plants: the margins of streams are always damp, and the most modest design will blend convincingly into its surroundings if you landscape it with marginal rocks and wetland plants. A regular gradient can be broken up by intermediate pools or a waterfall if these look appropriate.

SITE PREPARATION

Mark out the course in the same way as building a pond (see page 37), with levels if the fall is otherwise imperceptible, and then start digging at the bottom by excavating the collection pool. Use the removed soil to build up a bank or slope to enhance the gradient if necessary; otherwise keep it to one side for backfilling and landscaping the sides.

Continue digging out and building up the full length of the course. Ensure the cavity is deep enough to accommodate any essential foundation or underlay, depending on the construction material you decide to use (see below). Test the fall of each stretch with a plank and spirit level. This is especially important where a gentle consistent slope is needed. Check levels from side to side, to make sure that lateral loss of water is avoided.

MAKING THE WATERCOURSE

Materials used to build ponds are also suitable for watercourses, with the exception of clay, which is too easily eroded and difficult to keep watertight.

Flexible liner
This can be adapted to almost any design, formal or naturalistic. The amount needed is calculated in the same way as for a pond (see page 40), allowing an extra 8cm (3in) minimum along each side for bedding into the banks. If more than one strip is used the strips should be overlapped by about 8cm (3in) if the pieces are joined with a mastic-type adhesive, or at least 15cm (6in) if they are not glued together.

Excavate the channel, with an extra 2.5cm (1in) to allow for an underlining of felt or loft insulation or 5cm (2in) if you are using soft sand. Also take out enough soil along

With a little ingenuity water's inevitable downhill progress can be harnessed to create imaginative features, such as this channel lined with concrete and pebbles and cut through a pavement of immaculately shaped slabs (left) or the tiers of plain gully sections laid as a lively stepped cataract (right).

the sides if you are including a formal edging with its finished surface at ground level.

Remove all large or sharp stones, evenly spread the underlining and then start laying the liner from the bottom upwards. Smooth the sheet into place and anchor its edges on the banks with a few stones. Overlap the next strip over the lower piece and continue laying until you reach the top.

Test the lie and gradient of the course by running some water from the top. If you are satisfied, bury the edges under soil, stones or turf. The bed of formal and gently inclined courses can be covered with gravel, pebbles or slate chippings to hide the liner, and larger stones can be added to modulate the flow (see box page 69).

Concrete

Concrete is an excellent material for making stream beds that does not need a smooth finish – roughly sculpted areas quickly blend and weather to a natural look. It is important to limit the slope of banks to about forty-five degrees or less to prevent the wet mixture from slipping, or you can use shuttering to support steeper sides while the concrete sets.

Dig out the course about 15cm (6in) deeper than the finished dimensions, and lay a 5–8cm (2–3in) bed of builder's sand over the area.

Start concreting from one end, emptying the mix into the bottom of the channel and gradually trowelling it up the sides to give an 8cm- (3in-) thick layer all over.

Wait a few hours for the mix to go off and then add any rocks and gravel, pressing these into the surface enough to anchor them.

Protect the surface from rain and hot sun, and leave for ten to fourteen days to harden. Finish off the edges with soil or turf. Flush the stream thoroughly with water before adding plants.

Pre-formed units

These are rigid modular sections moulded in plastic or fibreglass, and may be finished in a variety of textured surfaces to make them look more natural. Although still artificial in appearance, their hard outlines can be disguised with marginal rocks or plants and a submerged layer of gravel to suggest an authentic stream bed. They are usually supplied in short convenient lengths, designed to overlap or link to intermediate pools for a longer run.

Mark out the stream course using the units as templates (see page 40).

Left Large volumes of water gushing down a complex series of stone ledges can produce the constantly moist environment needed to support such an exuberant plant collection.

Right Even a functional land-drain outlet can be incorporated into a garden plan to refresh the surroundings with sound and humidity.

Dig out the channel, making it 8cm (3in) deeper and 15cm (6in) wider than the units to accommodate the underlining.

Spread an 8cm (3in) layer of builder's sand over the floor and sides of the channel; use loft insulation blanket instead for steeper sides.

Starting from the bottom, nestle each unit into the underlining, making sure it is firm and level from side to side – add or remove sand to adjust the fit. Check overlaps fit well as you go.

Pack loose fine soil into any spaces at the sides, test for levels once more, and then run some water in at the top to approve the flow before finishing and naturalizing the edges.

WATERFALLS

These have a unique fascination and are great favourites for including in any watercourse or as lively features on their own. Depending on the volume of water and the height from which it tumbles, you can produce a soothing

Adjusting velocity

Size of pump is one influence on the rate of flow; the other is the configuration of the stream bed. Halving its depth or width will double the water speed – use gravel on the bottom and stones at the sides of the bed to adjust the flow in this way. Positioning a few stones in the middle of the bed will give the impression of greater speed. Choose smooth rounded stones where they are in contact with a liner, or alternatively bed them securely in concrete.

whisper or the thunder of a cataract in full spate. Beware of over-enthusiasm, though: falling water can be insistent and distracting and you may not enjoy being roared about on every side by a tidal wave of sound, although this can be a useful way to cancel intrusive background noise such as the drone of traffic.

A waterfall may consist of a single ledge of any height or width to suit the style and gradient of the site, or a cascade, comprising a number of terraced steps with water dropping a short distance from one to the next. Much of a fall's impact depends on the sill or lip over which the water flows: letting it project over the pool below amplifies sound and movement, whereas reducing the overhang softens the effect. With no sill at all, water will spill almost silently over the edge. The width of the sill can be a critical influence on the rate of flow and thus the size of pump (see box).

The same construction materials can be used for waterfalls as for streams.

Concrete is easily sculpted into random free forms, with the opportunity of permanently bedding in stones and sills.

Flexible liners easily mould themselves to informal layouts but you need to engineer the sills carefully, either by moulding the soil and underlining to shape or by wrapping the liner round rocks or treated timber to make distinct ledges.

Pre-formed units are available to build a complete system of header pool, linked waterfall modules and a catchment basin at the foot of the layout.

FOUNTAINS

A fountain will animate any kind of pond – formal or informal – and can also introduce moving water as a small self-contained feature in otherwise dry garden designs, even indoors. All types have the same basic components: a head unit that includes the selected style of (often adjustable) jet, an electric pump that is usually coupled directly to the base of the head unit, and a reservoir tank in which the pump is submerged.

Styles range widely from sculpted centrepieces and proud elaborate plumes that would add grandeur to a large pond to the tiniest bubbling spring that can fit easily into a pot, tub or bed of pebbles. Choose a kind that

A bubble fountain is a safe and charming device for introducing fluid movement, especially when multiplied, as here, into a major ornamental feature.

complements its setting, ideally placed prominently on its own because a fountain is a focal point designed to play to an audience, unlike other water features which need to blend comfortably into their surroundings.

Most fountains operate vertically, projecting water with varying degrees of force up into the air, but the same mechanical principle can be adapted for a wall-mounted spout (which is possibly the safest water feature where small children are likely to play). In its simplest form the pump sits in a tank, above or below ground, and drives water up a delivery pipe to the spout, where it can gush from a tap, gargoyle or similar ornament and fall back into the tank through a grille that is often disguised with pebbles.

Design principles

Expect a small feature like a bubble fountain to need a flow rate of about 450 litres (100 gallons) per hour, fountains at least 675 litres (150 gallons) per hour.

Keep a sense of proportion and adjust the spray height of a fountain to less than half the width of the pond.

A small submerged pump and reservoir are sufficient to power a bubble fountain, which can be incorporated into a variety of attractive garden ornaments such as a classic stone sphere (left) or a terracotta urn (right), changing their colours and textures with a constant film of flowing water.

Increase the flow of water by keeping delivery pipes as short, straight and wide as possible.

Smaller features work successfully with low-voltage pumps, a useful safety consideration.

Coarse droplets are more eye-catching than a fine spray, especially if backlit to improve their sparkle.

Remember that few plants appreciate being constantly splashed, whereas fish benefit from the turbulence, which adds extra oxygen to the water.

Making a bubble fountain

Millstone, pebble and bubble fountains are variations on the same method of constructing a small free-standing feature, using a pump submerged in a water reservoir that may be buried or set above ground. This reservoir may be a purpose-made chamber, a tub, half-barrel or dustbin, or a circular hole excavated in the ground and fitted with a flexible liner.

Dig out a cavity large enough to hold the tank flush with the ground, or about 90cm (3ft) across and 60cm (2ft) deep for a flexible liner.

Gardeners are fortunate in that essential natural materials such as water and foliage readily marry in designs with all kinds of hard landscaping ingredients, such as stone, earthenware, stainless steel and ceramics.

Plants for splash zones

The area close to a waterfall is hostile to most flowering plants because pollen is easily damaged by water, as are many kinds of foliage if constantly wet and exposed to the percussive effect of spray and falling water. Plants that tolerate these conditions include mosses, which are typical headwater plants able to find a purchase for their roots on slippery stones. Ferns such as forms of *Athyrium*, *Matteuccia*, *Onoclea*, *Pilularia*, *Salvinia* and *Thelypteris* are happy in misty spray, as are grassy-leaved plants ('monocots') like sedges, rushes and true grasses such as the lovely cotton grass (*Eriophorum angustifolium*) and purple moor grass (*Molinia caerulea* 'Variegata'), both of which prefer acid soil or water.

Fit the tank or liner in place and install an electric pump centrally on the floor of the chamber. Choose a model capable of moving about 450 litres (100 gallons) per hour.

Use a panel of stout welded mesh to cover the chamber, supported on treated timber battens across larger cavities. Feed the pump cable and delivery pipe through the mesh.

Attach the fountain head to the delivery pipe just above the mesh, and then covered it with cobble stones, pebbles or a similar attractive disguise.

If you are installing a millstone take care to support its heavy weight: set it on brick or block pillars built inside the tank or chamber, or adapt a cavity in the ground to include a shelf running all round the perimeter about 15cm (6in) wide and 8–10cm (3–4in) deep. Make sure the stone sits absolutely level and leave a 2.5–5cm (1–2in) gap round its rim for water to drain back into the reservoir.

PLAYING WITH WATER

Few can resist the appeal of water as it chuckles over stones or insinuates its way down a path of least resistance. Its playful character can be captured in a range of entertaining, even whimsical features used as additions or alternatives to the basic set pieces like a pond or stream. Remember only that your arrangement

Multi-coloured shingle (left) and gleaming slate fragments (right) are just two of the many attractive kinds of loose aggregate that can be used to conceal the pump and reservoir at the mechanical heart of every garden fountain.

must have a source, an outlet and efficient containment to prevent lateral loss into the soil, unless this is used to irrigate a marsh, water meadow or bog garden.

Types of jet

- Spray: a simple arching shower from one or more jets, usually falling in a regular circle.
- Tiered: a complex spray in several layers and falling in concentric circles.
- Bubble: a gentle erratic froth of agitated water for pebble fountains and millstones
- Geyser: a more powerful bubble jet producing a foaming column of water.
- Bell: an almost unchanging hemisphere of water that sparkles but rarely splashes.
- Tulip: a more sophisticated version of the bell jet with a distinct column or 'stem'.

Laminated pergola piers cascade with water pumped up their centres, enhancing the rich colours of timber and stone and refreshing the surrounding plants with a cool rain of moisture.

Off-centre often best

There is an understandable temptation to position any fountain centrally but this can look rather obvious, unless total formality is intended, and can disturb the entire pond, reducing opportunities for growing surface plants, most of which can be injured if their leaves are permanently wet. Setting the fountain to one side is more imaginative and will then divide the pond into two habitats: a still area and a splash zone.

You can play games with rainwater, for example, by conducting it from guttering into a down pipe that ends in a canal or basin, or in a hopper supplying the next drainage section. By fixing the outlet some distance from its destination the water will splash or gush from the pipe with a cadence that can be adjusted by directing it on to a large rock or into a ringing metal container. As an alternative source of water, arrange the overflow from a water butt to feed surplus rainwater into your system.

A simple channel can be a great source of pleasure, and may be static – self-contained and topped up occasionally with a canful of clean water saved indoors – or move placidly from end to end, driven by a small submerged pump. The channel might run across a patio, like a drainage gully, or surround it with a necklace of water. It could accompany a path down the garden or sit on the top of a low wall like a fluid coping for you to dabble your fingers in.

CONTAINERS

Bowls and basins of all kinds have an Oriental nuance and, even when small, can refresh the air with coolness and negative ions. Try placing them like finger bowls beside entrances and gateways so that they can be appreciated by birds and visitors alike. Where a gutter drips or water trickles from the top of a wall, suspend a chain to guide it to refill a basin placed strategically

A natural and freely available plant product, bamboo has instant appeal and when hollowed out it is a favourite means of delivering water in traditional Japanese gardening, usually in the form of a simple waterspout feeding a stone or wooden container, as in these examples.

Plants for a bamboo water feature

Ferns, small bamboos, ornamental grasses, reeds and sedges all look authentic. Fine examples include *Dryopteris affinis*, *Matteuccia struthiopteris*, *Fargesia murieliae* 'Novocento' and *F. nitida*, *Pleioblastus auricomus* and *P. fortunei*, *Typha minima*, *Cyperus involucratus* 'Nanus' and *Hakonechloa macra*.

underneath. In the evening float nightlights on the surface to glimmer in the twilight like fireflies.

Cast-off containers can make inspired water features if set over a hidden tank and pump: a punctured watering can, rusty jug or tilted flower pot can be fitted to the end of the delivery pipe, sealed all round with silicon to make a watertight connection, and then angled to spill quietly back into the reservoir below. Water can be delivered to the container from above by an arrangement of hollow bamboo poles, as in the classic Japanese waterspout or deer scarer (shishi-odoshi).

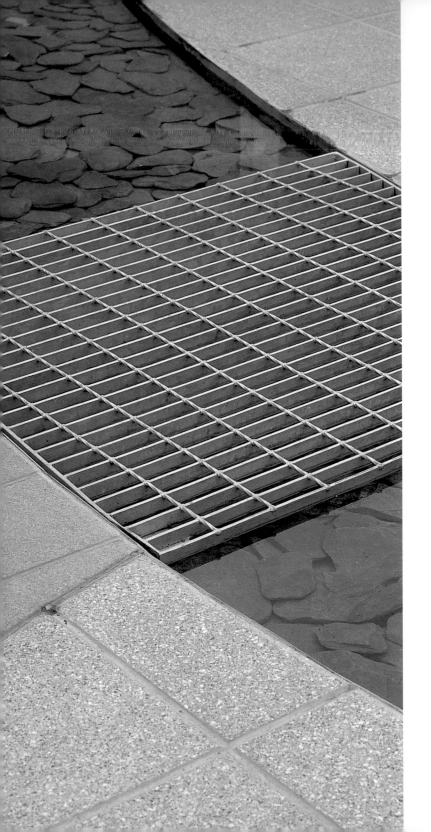

Crossing water is compulsive. This metal grille (left) complements the uncompromising paved surroundings and ensures safe dry passage, while the more elaborate timber decking (right) is somewhere to linger and look in the pond depths or play Pooh sticks in moving water.

ACCESSORIES

Various secondary features will suggest themselves once your design is complete and functioning. Two particularly sympathetic additions that can be modified to suit the scale of the watercourse are stepping stones and a bridge.

Stepping stones

These provide an inviting way to cross a stream with more intimate contact with the water, but you need to follow some simple guidelines.

For safety do not build them in deep water – the shallowest film can still suggest adventure and create fascinating eddies and ripples.

Space them no further than about 50cm (20in) between centres, enough for an easy stride.

Stones should be at least 38–40cm (15–16in) across, level and completely stable.

Concrete, stone and treated wood are all suitable. Nail wire netting to timber surfaces for a good foothold.

Bridges

There are timber bridge kits of various sizes for home assembly or you can build your own with materials that suit the surroundings – often the more satisfying plan for smaller streams. A stone slab mortared at both ends or a sturdy treated board securely pegged to each bank will often be adequate. More elaborate structures need careful selection to avoid upsetting the scale and balance of the setting, and you should consider installing handrails if people are likely to linger while crossing.

Bed stones in concrete or on two to three thicknesses of carpet underlay or loft insulation to avoid damaging flexible liners.

4

PLANTING up a POND

Plants are essential components of all but the smallest and most basic or minimalist ponds. They have a positive influence on water quality while also adding colour, beauty and an air of maturity to new ponds, helping them merge easily into their surroundings. Some species like to stand knee-deep in water, while others prefer just to dip their toes. The choice of plants to grow depends primarily on the type of habitat your pond has to offer.

For most gardeners a water feature is an opportunity to grow some of the countless lovely moisture-loving plants, whether in a varied and ambitious wetland scheme (previous pages) or a more secluded corner (left). Water lilies (*Nymphaea* species and cultivars, right) are firm favourites

PLACES FOR PLANTS

Water plants have evolved an exceptional ability to tolerate moisture in the soil. Some kinds simply react badly to dry conditions and have a preference for consistently wet boggy ground or the damp banks of water bodies, while often resenting deeper submersion. Some have specialized in surviving airless and waterlogged conditions by using their roots mainly for anchorage deep under water while their foliage floats at the surface, drawing oxygen from the air and nutrients from the water. Others have completely abandoned a settled existence and float freely with roots and even foliage completely submerged. Each of these different kinds has a preferred habitat and niche in the pond community, and an important role to play in a well-organized water world.

Deep-water aquatics
These are generally large plants that need a depth of about 23cm (9in) or more to develop fully. Their floating

foliage, which can spread to at least twice the depth at which they grow, helps to shade large areas of a pond, while their vigorous growth rate absorbs large amounts of nitrogen from the water, competing aggressively with floating algae for this nutrient and so preventing the water from turning green. Most ponds will have room only for two or three of these strong plants.

The numberous water lily culltivars are the best-known examples in this group, but there are many others. Outstanding kinds include:

- Water hawthorn (*Aponogeton distachyos*): oval speckled leaves and white, very fragrant flowers.
- Japanese pond lily (*Nuphar japonicum*): shiny spear-shaped leaves and yellow 'buttercups'.
- Water fringe (*Nymphoides peltata*): heart-shaped foliage and yellow-fringed blooms.
- Golden club (*Orontium aquaticum*): rosettes of waxy leaves and white flower spikes with golden tips.
- Water crowfoot (*Ranunculus aquatilis*): grassy submerged leaves, clover-like foliage on the surface and single white blooms; a good oxygenator (see page 96).

A selection that includes several marginal species such as flowering rush (*Butomus umbellatus*, right) plus a few deeper-water aquatics like the intriguing golden club (*Orontium aquaticum*, left) will provide the main ingredients of an effective planting scheme.

Marginal plants

These may behave like shallow-water aquatics, growing at depths up to about 15–20cm (6–8in), or moisture-loving terrestrial plants to grow in the mud at the water's edge. Possibly the most important landscape plants for ponds, they can be massed in lavish wild and informal schemes as a continuous border to disguise the frontier between land and water, or as solitary specimens to place judiciously around a formal pond. Submerged specimens are usually grown in baskets to control their spread, although their unconfined roots are good for stabilizing pond and stream banks when planted direct in soil.

Marginals for formal ponds

- Variegated sweet flag (*Acorus calamus* 'Variegatus'): cream-striped 'iris' leaves and yellowish flower spikes.
- Flowering rush (*Butomus umbellatus*): slim foliage and large rosy flower heads.
- Bog arum (*Calla palustris*): neat heart-shaped leaves, white flower spathes and red berries.

- Scouring rush (*Equisetum hyemale*): stiff rod-like stems with knuckles and prominent tips.
- Manna grass (*Glyceria maxima* var. *variegata*): yellow and white striped perennial grass.
- Japanese water iris (*Iris laevigata*): clumps of sword-shaped leaves and complex blue and yellow flowers.

Marginals for informal ponds
- Kingcups (*Caltha palustris*): dark foliage and early bright yellow flowers.

- Cardinal flower (*Lobelia cardinalis*): bronze foliage and rich red flower spikes.
- Water forget-me-not (*Myosotis scorpioides*): 'Mermaid' produces masses of pale blue flowers.
- Amphibious bistort (*Persicaria amphibia*): evergreen foliage and dense red flower spikes.
- Pickerel weed (*Pontederia cordata*): rich green spears and tight, gloriously blue flower spikes.
- Arrowhead (*Sagittaria sagittifolia*): arrow-shaped leaves and spikes of white flowers with dark centres.

Vivid spring-flowering kingcups or marsh marigolds (*Caltha palustris*, far left) and the distinctive arrowhead (*Sagittaria* species, left) are both nonchalant marginals for planting up the banks of informal wildlife and natural ponds (right).

Pontederia cordata or pickerel weed (left) is one of the most dependable and well-behaved marginals for ponds of all sizes, and flowers late, a month or two after *Persicaria* (syn. *Polygonum*) *bistorta* (right), which is a non-invasive knotweed that revels in bog garden conditions.

Plants that need caution

Some lovely marginals are invasive if allowed to spread freely and are best confined to baskets to prevent them from overwhelming less robust neighbours. Beware if you grow greater spearwort (*Ranunculus lingua*), *Houttuynia cordata*, plain green water grass (*Glyceria maxima*), sweet galingale (*Cyperus longus*), lizard's tail (*Saururus cernuus*), water mint (*Mentha aquatica*) and larger forms of reedmace (*Typha* species or 'bulrushes'), unless you have plenty of space or the determination to trim their spread ruthlessly. Himalayan balsam (*Impatiens glandulifera*) is a stately and handsome annual that self-seeds liberally and can be invasive, especially once loose in the wild.

Water- and bog-garden plants display some of the most dramatically varied foliage, from the intricate symmetry of fern fronds and emphatically spiky clumps of grasses, reeds and irises (right), to hostas' shapely corpulence and (far right) the arresting extravagance of prickly rhubarb (*Gunnera manicata*), a giant among hardy bog plants.

Bog plants

There is a huge range of perennials that dislike standing water and waterlogged ground but grow best where the soil is permanently moist. Species include grasses, sedges and reeds, wildflowers and many cultivated garden plants that often grow more vigorously and happily in the wet borderland between pond and garden than in a conventional herbaceous border (for bog garden construction and planting, see page 102).

Floaters

These plants float at or just below the surface of still water, with their roots trailing freely and absorbing dissolved nutrients. They are a vital component of the pond plant community, supporting deep-water aquatics in their role of surface cover plants. They add charm and diversity as their clumps and rosettes congregate into rafts of foliage and flowers, drifting into favoured parts of the pond. Some are hardy perennials, while others come from warm climates and in frost-prone areas are added to the pond in spring and overwintered indoors. Individual

The most outstanding sculptural plants, such as tender and potentially invasive water hyacinths (*Eichornia crassipes*, left) and the various graceful species of *Cyperus* (right), merit growing in isolation as star specimens.

plants are simply dropped on to the surface and left to drift and multiply. Popular kinds include:

- Water hyacinth (*Eichornia crassipes*): tender but vigorous (invasive in warm waters); shiny succulent foliage and sprays of bold lavender and yellow blooms.
- Frogbit (*Hydrocharis morsus-ranae*): hardy and restrained, producing bright white and yellow flowers and foliage like a small water lily.
- Water lettuce (*Pistia stratiotes*): a tender perennial that makes tidy rosettes of velvety, square-ended leaves.
- Water soldier (*Stratiotes aloides*): spiky semi-evergreen tufts, rising or sinking according to season and growth stage.
- Water chestnut (*Trapa natans*): a tender annual with pretty rosettes of angular, stippled leaves; flowers and fruits only in hot climates.
- Bladderwort (*Utricularia vulgaris*): hardy carnivorous plant, with a floating mass of threads and bladders under the surface and golden yellow pouched flowers.

Oxygenators

These essential utilitarian plants stay submerged for most

of their lives, rooting into baskets or marginal mud and regulating the pond chemistry by supplying the water with oxygen while removing carbon dioxide and surplus minerals. Various species are available, usually mixed in bunches of cuttings bound together by weighted clips so that the plants sink when tossed into the pond. Alternatively plant several bunches in a basket and lower this to the bottom (see page 102).

Common kinds include pondweed, both curled (*Potamogeton crispus*) and fennel-leaved (*P. pectinatus*), hairgrass (*Eleocharis acicularis*), water starwort (*Callitriche hermaphroditica*) and spiked milfoil (*Myriophyllum spicatum*). For larger, well-established ponds choose more vigorous species such as goldfish weed (*Lagarosiphon major*), Canadian pondweed (*Elodea canadensis*), hornwort (*Ceratophyllum demersum*), water violet (*Hottonia palustris*) and water crowfoot (*Ranunculus aquatilis*).

PLANNING FOR PLANTING

Each of the different plant types makes a distinct contribution to the health of the pond as a flourishing ecosystem. Ideally members from each group should be included in your planting plan so that a balanced water community develops, but space limitations may prevent this. It is easy to overcrowd plants with consequent losses, so match plant numbers to the available water surface area and marginal planting space.

Different water species are easily combined to make varied and appealing partnerships. The contrasting forms of pond weeds, ferns and the striped spikes of zebra rush (*Schoenoplectus lacustris* subsp. *tabernaemontani* 'Zebrinus', left) blend busily in a miniature water garden, whereas lily pads, reeds and expansive ornamental rhubarb (*Rheum palmatum* cultivars, right) make a more placid composition.

Pondweeds for bowls

As their name implies, pondweeds can be invasive and defy attempts to control them in a pond environment where an ample supply of space and dissolved nutrients can support explosive growth. Some kinds make attractive miniature floating plants for bowls and basins, however, where their dainty structure is more easily appreciated. Ivy-leaved duckweed (*Lemna trisulca*) resembles a mat of tiny stars and multiplies at a more modest rate than its weedier relatives. Fairy moss (*Azolla filiculoides*) is a pretty fern barely 1cm (1/2in) across that floats in lacy rafts, turns red in cold weather and passes winter as dormant submerged buds. Keep this species out of large ponds and natural watercourses, where it can multiply alarmingly.

Examples of appropriate populations

- Small pond (about 0.75 sq.m/8 sq.ft): 5 oxygenators, 2 floaters, 4 marginals.
- Medium pond (about 1.8 sq.m/20 sq.ft): 10 oxygenators, 3 floaters, 6 marginals, 2 deep-water aquatics.
- Large pond (about 4.5 sq.m/50 sq.ft): 20 oxygenators, 5 floaters, 8 marginals, 3 deep-water aquatics.

As well as matching quantities to space, consider the character of the site and your own preferences regarding its finished appearance.

If the pond is intended for fish or wildlife make sure that between one- and two-thirds of the surface is covered with floating foliage for shade and seclusion.

The surface of reflective pools should be kept clear. Increase the number of submerged plants to maintain water quality.

Formal ponds look best with well-spaced plants in patterns or as isolated groups and individuals.

Integrate informal ponds with their setting by planting generous zones of bog plants and marginals.

Concentrate on native flowers for wildlife ponds, including some berried shrubs and tall-stemmed plants for emerging pond creatures.

Choose a selection of plants for colour and interest at each of the seasons, and take sunny or shady aspects into account.

Making a planting diagram

Draw a scale plan of the pond and its surroundings, together with existing plants and features. Mark possible planting sites (to scale) and label them with the type of plant to grow there.

Compile a list of plants you would like, dividing them into water and waterside species. Annotate each with its height, spread, appearance and flowering season, and the kind of conditions it prefers.

Include some evergreens for all-year performance and enough marginals to fill about one-third of the perimeter (they will increase to cover a larger area). Finally match plants to marked sites, remembering the need for a satisfactory balance and appearance when plants mature.

HOW TO PLANT IN WATER

Marginal and deep-water aquatics may be planted in baskets, which will limit spread and make maintenance easier, or direct into a layer of soil, which supports more vigorous and often healthier growth (covering a synthetic liner with soil can also protect it from the ageing effects of light). Which method you choose depends on the type of pond and the amount of water gardening you are prepared to do. As a compromise you could grow deep-water plants in baskets so that they are easily lifted out for cleaning or propagation, while growing marginals in

Deep-water aquatics such as these water lilies (left) are usually grown in baskets sitting on the pond floor, whereas marginals prefer the shallower immersion provided by growing them on a submerged shelf around the pond sides (right; left foreground).

A planting shelf

Submerged shelves round all or part of a pond's margin are ideal for plants that prefer to grow in shallow water. Pre-formed liners often include these, or you can make provision for one or more while excavating the profile for a pond made with concrete or a flexible liner. About 23cm (9in) is a practical width, while the depth can be 20–30cm (8–12in) below the surface; use the same measurements when constructing several shelves of increasing depth.

shallower water in a layer of soil spread on a shelf around the pond edge.

Direct planting

Use ordinary clean garden soil that is not too fertile – subsoil is often ideal and can moderate growth as well as excessive nutrient transfer into the water. Sieve out and discard stones, sticks and larger organic fragments, and spread the soil 10–15cm (4–6in) deep over the bottom of the pond or just on marginal shelves. A covering of pea gravel will stabilize the soil against disturbance by fish or moving water. When filling the pond rest the end of the hosepipe in a container or on a sack to avoid stirring up the soil.

Use the same soil mix or a proprietary aquatic compost when planting. To plant direct into a soil bottom, centre a heavy stone on a square of hessian sacking and pack the planting mix all round the roots to make a ball 15–20cm (6–8in) across when the sacking is wrapped up around the neck of the plant. Tie loosely with string, then lower the parcel into the water and let it sink to the bottom.

Planting in baskets

Growing plants in perforated baskets allows you to remove them easily for care and inspection, and limits the spread of more energetic species.

Line the basket with hessian sacking or plastic micromesh, partly fill with soil or compost, and position the plant so that its neck or rootstock is just below the surface.

Pack the soil firmly all round and finish with a 2.5cm (1in) mulch of pea gravel or shingle to prevent disturbance.

Water thoroughly and then lower the basket carefully into place, pausing until air bubbles cease before releasing it.

In deep water stand the basket on bricks until new leaves reach the surface; then lower it by removing bricks (in stages if necessary) until the plant is at its ideal depth.

A GARDEN FOR BOG PLANTS

A bog garden is a special wet bed or border where moisture-loving plants and many marginals can find the conditions they prefer. Naturally boggy ground may be suitable without further amendment apart from basic cultivation, but very often the site needs special preparation as an area where the pond can overflow or as a separate wetland feature in dry surroundings.

You will need to impede drainage in some way so that the bog garden remains consistently moist.

If you are relying on water from the pond to maintain soil moisture levels, the usual method is to dig out an area about 30cm (12in) deep immediately next to the

Water supplies an equally
effective setting for wild and
natural plant populations
and more consciously
artistic landscapes such as
this almost dream-like
composition of rocks,
twining stems, elegant
foliage and exotic blooms.

pond excavation. Leave a wall between the two cavities 5cm (2in) lower than the rest of the pond margin. Line the bog site with a flexible liner, tucked under the pond's liner where they meet. Use a knife to perforate the sides of the liner at 90cm (3ft) intervals (except the side next to the pond), and then spread a 5cm (2in) layer of grit or gravel over the bottom before filling with good garden soil free from all perennial weed roots.

The same method can be adapted for a free-standing bog garden. Leave the liner unpunctured and bury a perforated irrigation pipe in the layer of gravel at the bottom. Stop the pipe at one end, connect a hosepipe coupling to the other, and then spread a sheet of woven plastic matting on top to keep the soil from infiltrating the grit and pipework. After planting keep the bed heavily mulched with garden compost or shredded bark to discourage evaporation and maintain evenly moist conditions.

Preparing a new bog garden

Weeds are often difficult to remove from wet ground, where they may be lush and tenacious, so clear the soil of weed roots as meticulously as you can before planting. To help retain moisture fork in plenty of organic material, adding up to one-third by volume of garden compost or well-rotted manure. Treading on the prepared soil during planting can cause compaction and airlessness: avoid this by standing on a board to help spread your weight.

The *Iris* genus supplies probably the largest and most exciting range of bulbs and bulb-like plants for the water garden, including the flamboyant race of Japanese flags (*Iris ensata*, syn. *I. kaempferi*), among them this popular cultivar 'Rose Queen' (right).

Water plants thoroughly before and after planting.

Common perennials that revel in bog gardens include astilbes, cardinal flower (*Lobelia cardinalis*), day lilies (*Hemerocallis*), eupatoriums, globe flower (*Trollius*), goat's beard (*Aruncus*), gunnera, hostas, kingcups (*Caltha*), ligularias, loosestrife (*Lythrum*), mimulus, primulas and rodgersias.

LOOKING AFTER A WATER GARDEN

A balanced and established water garden will become self-regulating in many respects, and caring for a pond and its inhabitants round the year is less demanding than some other areas of the garden.

How much maintenance you have to do varies with the type of water feature. Deposits of scum and algae can build up in bowls, basins and still pools without plants, and these may need emptying and scrubbing clean once or twice a year. A wildlife pond, on the other hand, can be allowed to accumulate plant growth and bottom

Bulbs for moist soils

Although most bulbs and bulb-like plants prefer good drainage, a few species have adapted to survival in damp or wet marginal ground and look very handsome near water, where their emphatic leaf shapes and sometimes arching flower stems produce exciting reflections. Plants to try include arum lilies (*Zantedeschia*), angel's fishing rods (*Dierama*), snake's-head fritillary (*Fritillaria meleagris*), snowflakes (*Leucojum*), hoop-petticoat daffodils (*Narcissus bulbocodium*) and many irises, especially *Iris ensata* and *I. sibirica*.

debris as part of its natural evolution, and may be left undisturbed for ten years or more before needing some sensitive restoration.

Following a few simple guidelines can simplify pond care and help prevent problems.

- Do not use chemical fertilizers or pesticides, as these can be detrimental to pond life and water quality.
- Stretch netting over ponds in the autumn to catch falling tree leaves (spread these among bog garden plants) and prevent them from sinking and fouling the water.
- Clear dying plant material from the pond, but do not cut down dead marginal stems until spring as they protect dormant roots and supply wildlife cover.
- Remove tender pond plants in autumn for overwintering in a bowl of water indoors or somewhere frost-free.
- Mulch bog gardens and beds of marginals with garden compost every spring to control weeds and supply slow-release nutrients.

Green water

Ponds often turn green in late spring as increasing warmth and sunlight fuel the rapid growth of aquatic algae, which feed on the dissolved minerals that often arrive in water draining from the surrounding soil or in tap water used to top up levels. This is a natural, though disfiguring, phenomenon that often stabilizes itself later in the season.

You can reduce the problem by including plenty of submerged oxygenating plants, shading part of the surface from sunlight with floating foliage, and stocking the pond with snails and freshwater mussels, which feed on algae and filter the water.

More filamentous algae can develop into green mats of 'blanket weed'. Do not treat this with chemicals; it is easily dredged out with a lawn rake or twisted on to a rough stick for adding to the compost heap, or you can sink barley straw pads in the water as a natural form of discouragement.

- Clean, service and store pumps over winter, and replace with a pond heater where fish need ice-free conditions.
- Vigorous plants in baskets will need dividing and replanting every three to four years to rejuvenate them and prevent them from spreading beyond their confines.
- Thin floating plants if they cover more than two-thirds of the surface, and fish out blanket weed and other algae before they can take over (see box).

Restoring a neglected pond

A pond that is seriously overgrown, smelly or silted up will need complete or substantial overhaul. Formal ponds can usually be drained or pumped out for cleaning after checking whether any plants can be saved for propagation and replanting – keep these and any fish in large bowls of water until you are ready to return them to the renovated pond. Clear out any mud, wash down the sides and repair the liner if it is leaking (see below). When refilling, add samples of the original water for a basic stock of water organisms, together with a water conditioner if fish are to be reintroduced.

Informal and wildlife ponds need more cautious restoration to avoid disturbing or destroying a possibly huge and diverse population of plant and animal life. Autumn is the best time for the work, in between the usual breeding and hibernating seasons. Remove up to half the plant growth, leaving any from within the pond to drain on the bank for a day or two to allow creatures to return to the water. Bale or pump out about half the water and dredge out any silt and organic material from the bottom, but leave one or two areas undisturbed to restock the pond with organisms. Restore the water level by gently trickling in water from a hosepipe.

Repairing a pond leak

Age or injury can damage pond liners. The water may settle of its own accord to the level of the leak or you might have to drain or bale out the pond to expose the damage for inspection. Polythene liners have a very limited life and are best replaced altogether once they start to deteriorate; repair of other kinds is usually possible and simple to carry out.

Repair kits are available for rigid pre-formed liners, which eventually develop cracks, especially thinner types and those on unstable foundations.

Patching kits are used to repair butyl and PVC liners; clean the damaged area first to provide a good key for the waterproof adhesive.

Fine cracks in concrete can be treated with pond sealant or mastic cement. Wider fissures need chiselling out and filling with waterproof mortar.

Feeding plants

Established deep-water and marginal plants may need feeding when growth resumes in spring because nutrients easily leach from the soil or compost into the pond. Feed them cautiously to avoid enriching the water further and stimulating algal growth. Use a slow-release fertilizer applied direct to individual plants, and where possible choose one that is seaweed-based. Do not over-apply, and never feed floaters and submerged plants.

THE WATER GARDEN YEAR

Tending a water garden is simple and seasonal if you follow this checklist of essential care.

Spring

- Cut down and clear dead top growth; renew overgrown plants by division or cuttings.
- Feed established water lilies by burying sachets of specialist slow-release fertilizer close to the crowns.
- Late in the season introduce new fish and tender water plants overwintered indoors.
- Start feeding fish, lightly at first and increasing as they become more active.
- Start treating green water and other multiplying algae (see opposite).

At the height of a hot summer, a lightly shaded and densely planted pond can be a welcome cool and refreshing sanctuary away from the heat of the midday sun.

Summer

- Watch out for first signs of pests such as aphids and water lily beetles (see box).
- In sultry weather aerate fishponds by playing a jet of water on the surface; top up levels.
- Weed, mulch and, in a dry season, water the bog garden with a gently running hosepipe.
- Thin floating plants, reaching inaccessible groups with a sharp knife tied to the end of cane; remove the pruned material for composting.

Autumn

- Net the pond to catch falling tree leaves, and leave in place until winter.
- Continue topping up levels and removing algae wherever necessary.
- Protect tender plants against frost, where they grow or indoors; insulate sinks and tubs.
- Clean and store pumping equipment and install a pond heater where required.

Controlling pests

Insect pests are part of the natural cycle of growth, death and decay, and all plants are subject to them. Few problems will be serious, however, if you have maintained a balanced water world. Pests are themselves part of a food chain and a thriving pond will contain creatures that prey on them. Rather than resort to chemical insecticides, spray aphids, beetles and other pests forcefully with a hosepipe so that they are knocked into the water, where they will be eaten.

Winter

- Check that surfaces are not slippery to walk on: scrub greasy stonework and nail wire netting to timber walkways or paint in summer with sand and exterior adhesive.
- In prolonged cold weather remove some of the ice from fishponds less than 60cm (2ft) deep (do not break it forcefully as sudden percussion can stun fish).
- Reduce the feeding of fish according to their amount of activity.

INDEX

Page numbers in *italics* refer to captions to the illustrations